HAWAII VOLCANOES

National Park

by Ruth Radlauer

**Photographs by
Ed and Ruth Radlauer**

**Design and map by
Rolf Zillmer**

AN ELK GROVE BOOK

 CHILDRENS PRESS, CHICAGO

Every national park is a BEQUEST OF BEAUTY,
a gift for those who follow.
It is a place of special interest or
beauty that has been set aside by the
United States government especially for you,
your children, and their great-great-grandchildren.
This bequest is yours to have and to care for,
so that others who follow can do the same
during their lives.

With gratitude to the personnel
of Hawai'i Volcanoes National Park

Photo credits:
Paul Banko, page 19
Richard Pultz, page 33 (eruption)
The following photographs were supplied
by the Hawai'i Natural History Association:
pages 5 (eruption), 31 by J. D. Griggs
page 13 by Larry Katahira
pages 27, 35 (eruption), 39 (pahoehoe),
45 (eruption) by Glen Kaye
Cover by Gil Sloper

Cover: Mauna Ulu, November, 1973

Library of Congress Cataloging in Publication Data

Radlauer, Ruth Shaw.
  Hawai'i Volcanoes National Park.
  (Parks for people)
  ''An Elk Grove book.''
  1. Hawaii Volcanoes National Park—Juvenile
literature. I. Radlauer, Edward. II. Zillmer,
Rolf. III. Title.
DU628.H33R32   919.6   78-19718
ISBN 0-516-07498-9

3 4 5 6 7 8 9 10 11 12 13 14 15 R 85 84 83 82 81 80

Contents

What is Hawai'i Volcanoes National Park?

Hawai'i Volcanoes National Park is a growing place of expectations. Every now and then Kilauea Volcano erupts. Lava flows out, adding a layer to the land. Less often, Mauna Loa sends red hot lava down its sides. When lava reaches the sea, it adds land to the big island of Hawai'i.

This park is the rich green of ferns and the bright red lehua blossoms of the 'ohi'a tree.

Hawai'i Volcanoes National Park is stories and legends. It's the sound of old Hawaiian songs and the thump of a stone pounding taro root to make food called *poi*.

At times your national park could be the tremble of the earth under your feet and a rumbling roar of a volcanic eruption. But most of the time it's the tremble of your expectations. Will Kilauea erupt while you're here? Will Mauna Loa make the island grow? One thing you can expect is to grow in your own understanding of the earth and its volcanoes.

Your understanding will grow much more if you learn how to ''speak Hawaiian'' and how to ''speak volcano.''

...aʻi, November, 1977

Hapuʻu—A Tree Fern

Ōhiʻa-Lehua Tree

Pounding Poi At Wahaʻula Heiau

How to "Speak Hawaiian"

Most people in Hawai'i speak English, but you'll hear Hawaiian words everywhere. "Aloha" is a word we all know. It means hello, farewell, goodwill, and love.

Many of the words may sound strange but beautiful. Written with the English alphabet, this lovely language has only 12 letters. The consonants are *h,k,l,m, n,p,* and *w.* These all sound the same as they do in English except that "w" sounds as "v" when it comes after "e" or "i." At the beginning of a word or after "a," "w" can have a "v" or "w" sound.

The vowels are *a,e,i,o,* and *u,* and sound like this:

a as in *saw*
e as in *grey*
i as in *machine*
o as in *no*
u as the *oo* in *moon.*

Sometimes the vowels pile up together in a word like "Kilauea." Say, "Kee lah oo ay ah," and run it all together.

When a vowel is repeated, as in the word, "hapu'u," you just say the sound twice: "hah poo oo." This symbol, ('), is called a glottal stop. Between two vowels in a word like "ama'u," it means a tiny voice pause, a glottal stop.

page 6

Here are a few Hawaiian words.

aa	rough, chunky lava
ahu	a pile of rocks to mark a trail or to serve as a monument
akua	a god
ali'i	chief
ama'u	a large fern native to Hawai'i
'apapane	honeycreeper bird with red feathers
hale	house
Haleakala	house of the sun
Halema'uma'u	summit crater of Kilauea Volcano
haole	foreigner, usually a white person
hapu'u	tree fern native to Hawai'i
Haumea	goddess, Mother Earth, Pele's mother
Hawai'i Loa	man who discovered Hawai'i
heiau	temple
'i'iwi	small bright red bird of honeycreeper family
iki	small
'ili-ahi	sandalwood
'ili'ili	small stones used to make smoother, level floor
'ilio	dog
kaha ki'i	petroglyphs
kahuna	priest
Kane	a demigod, one of Haumea's children
kapu	a forbidden act—taboo
kaulua	double-hulled canoe
keiki	baby or small child
Kia'i	overlook, bluff, watchman
Kilauea	active volcano on island of Hawai'i
Kilauea Iki	crater in the side, or flank of Kilauea Volcano
kipuka	older lava where soil has formed to support plants, surrounded by newer lava flow; a meadow
kona	leeward; facing direction of wind; in Hawai'i, west
Ku	(short for Ku'aha'ilo) a god, Father Sky, Pele's father
lauhala	pandanus or screwpine used as weaving material for baskets and hats
lehua	red blossoms of 'ohi'a tree—see 'ohi'a
lei	necklace or wreath made of flowers, leaves, shells, feathers, worn at special times
loa	long
Makali'i	group of stars also known as Pleiades or Seven Sisters
mana	sacred or magic power
mauna	mountain
Mauna Loa	active volcano on island of Hawai'i
mele	chant
moa	jungle fowl
mu'umu'u	formerly a woman's underslip, now any Hawaiian clothing for women
Na Maka	(short for Na Maka o Kaha'i) goddess of the sea, Pele's sister
nene	Hawaiian goose, Hawai'i state bird
niu	coconut
'ohana	family
'ohelo	small native shrub in cranberry family
'ohi'a	native Hawaiian tree with red blossoms—see lehua
'ohi'a-lehua	see 'ohi'a
pahoehoe	lava with smooth or ropelike surface
pali	cliff
palila	gray, yellow, and white bird of honeycreeper family with a short bill
Pele	goddess of fire, volcano goddess
poi	a basic Hawaiian food made from cooked taro root; also made from breadfruit
pua	flower
pua'a	pig
pu'u	hill
Pu'uloa	long hill
'uala	sweet potato
ulu	to grow
uluhe	a native Hawaiian fern called a healer fern because it restores soil
Waha'ula	red mouth
wahine	female

How to "Speak Volcano"

Many scientists have come to Hawai'i so they can study the volcanoes. As the scientists study and learn, they add new words to the language of volcanoes. Some Hawaiian words which have been added to the language are *aa, pahoehoe, Pele's tears,* and *Pele's hair.*

But most volcano words come from other languages, especially Latin. You've heard about *lava* and *cinder.* Page nine has more volcano words along with their meanings.

By learning some of these words before you visit Hawai'i Volcanoes National Park, you'll understand more of what you see along Crater Rim Drive and in the museum. You'll also enjoy the walks and talks more.

Maybe someday you'll be one of those scientists who study volcanoes, a volcanologist. Then you'll really "speak volanco." And who knows? A volcano may even "speak" to you.

aa	rough, chunky lava	pahoehoe	lava with a smooth or ropelike surface
active volcano	a volcano that still erupts	Pele's hair	volcanic glass, spun out by wind to look like hair
ash	fine-grained ejecta—see *ejecta*	Pele's tears	hardened lava droplets
blocks	jagged ejecta over 6.4 cm across	pumice	lava full of air holes caused by gas escaping when the lava was molten
bombs	smooth, rounded ejecta over 6.4 cm across	rift	a fractured area in earth's crust
breccia	a mass of jagged rock fragments banded together	rift zone	highly fractured belt on the side, or flank, of a volcano where most eruptions take place
caldera	a volcanic crater larger than 1.6 km across	scoria	cinder; slaggy ejecta that looks spongy
cascade	lava flowing down a cliff or steep hill	seismograph	instrument to measure earth movements
cinder	spongy bits of lava the size of a pea or larger	shield volcano	a domelike volcano with gentle sloping sides—Kilauea and Mauna Loa are shield volcanoes.
cinder cone	a cone-shaped hill of cinder piled up around a vent	spatter	very liquid ejecta that flatten when they hit the ground—They often stick together.
dormant volcano	a fairly active volcano in its quiet period	spatter cone	a pile of spatter built up into a cone shape
ejecta	volcanic fragments thrown out, or ejected, by explosion	steam vent	a fumarole
extinct volcano	a volcano not expected to erupt again	tremor	trembling of ground caused by movement of magma through volcanic passageways called conduits
fault	a break, or fracture, in the earth's crust—Both sides of the fault have moved in relation to each other.		
fumarole	a hole from which gases come from inside the earth	tuff	volcanic ash that has welded together
lapilli	ejecta from about .2 to 6.4 cm across—One is a *lapillus*.	vent	hole where lava comes out
lava	hot liquid rock at or close to earth's surface and its cooled, hardened products—see *magma*	volcano	a break or hole in the earth where magma flows out as lava; also the mound, hill, or mountain created by eruption of lava and ejecta
lava tube	natural tunnel in a lava flow caused by draining of the flow beneath a solid surface	volcanologist	scientist who studies volcanoes
magma	hot liquid rock; lava stored inside the earth		

Where is Hawai'i Volcanoes National Park?

Hawai'i Volcanoes National Park is on the biggest of all the islands that make up the state of Hawai'i. To get there, you take a plane to the middle of the Pacific Ocean. You can land at the cities of Kailua-Kona or Hilo. Then by car or bus, you go south from either city on Hawai'i Highway 11 to the park.

Many people visit the park for a few hours. Others stay at Volcano House or in free campgrounds as long as seven days.

You'll probably want to hike some of the trails. Rough lava trails wear out light tennis shoes and thongs. For safety, you'll want strong hiking shoes or boots. Weather at this elevation of 1200 meters can be hot, cold, or rainy, so be prepared. And since there is no water on the trails, you need one canteen per person as you hike.

Write the Superintendent, Hawai'i Volcanoes National Park, HI 96718, for information about campgrounds. You can reserve a room in the hotel or a cabin with use of showers by writing Volcano House at the same address.

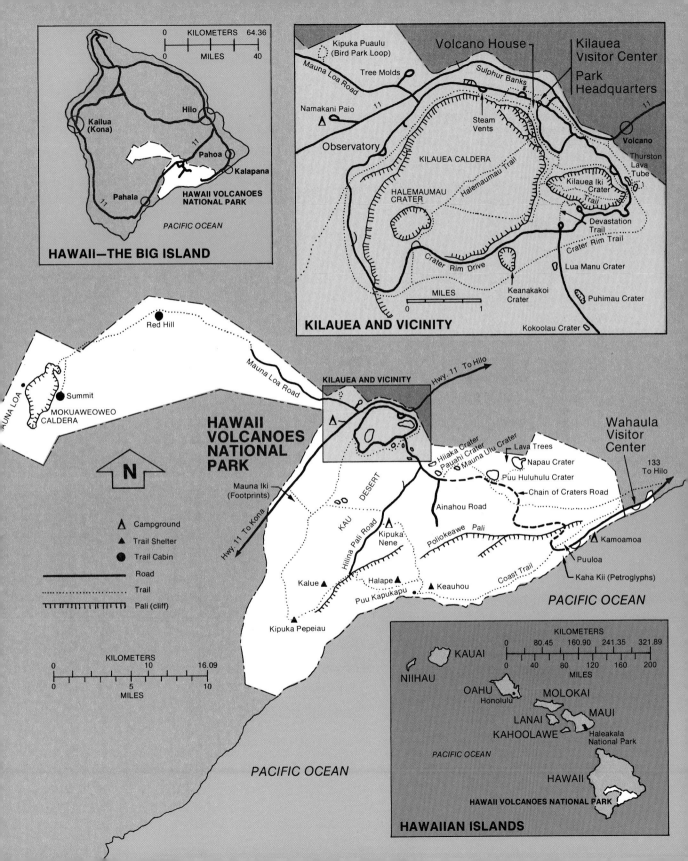

HAWAII—THE BIG ISLAND

KILOMETERS 64.36
MILES 40

Hilo
Kailua (Kona)
Pahoa
Kalapana
Pahala
11

HAWAII VOLCANOES NATIONAL PARK

PACIFIC OCEAN

KILAUEA AND VICINITY

Kipuka Puaulu (Bird Park Loop)
Volcano House
Kilauea Visitor Center
Park Headquarters
Mauna Loa Road
Tree Molds
Sulphur Banks
Namakani Paio
Steam Vents
Observatory
11
Volcano
Thurston Lava Tube
KILAUEA CALDERA
Kilauea Iki Crater
Halemaumau Trail
HALEMAUMAU CRATER
Kilauea Iki Trail
Devastation Trail
Crater Rim Trail
Crater Rim Drive
Lua Manu Crater
MILES 0 1
Keanakakoi Crater
Puhimau Crater
Kokoolau Crater

HAWAII VOLCANOES NATIONAL PARK

Red Hill
Mauna Loa Road
MAUNA LOA
Summit
MOKUAWEOWEO CALDERA
KILAUEA AND VICINITY
Hwy. 11 To Hilo
Hiiaka Crater
Pauahi Crater
Mauna Ulu Crater
Lava Trees
Napau Crater
Wahaula Visitor Center
133 To Hilo
Puu Huluhulu Crater
Mauna Iki (Footprints)
Chain of Craters Road
KAU
DESERT
Ainahou Road
N
Hwy. 11 To Kona
Kipuka Nene
Poliokeawe Pali
Kamoamoa
Hilina Pali Road
Puuloa
Kalue
Halape
Keauhou
Coast Trail
Kaha Kii (Petroglyphs)
Puu Kapukapu
PACIFIC OCEAN
Kipuka Pepeiau

△ Campground
▲ Trail Shelter
● Trail Cabin
——— Road
········· Trail
⊥⊥⊥⊥⊥ Pali (cliff)

KILOMETERS
0   10   16.09
0   5   10
MILES

PACIFIC OCEAN

HAWAIIAN ISLANDS

KILOMETERS
0   80.45 160.90 241.35 321.89
0   40   80   120   160   200
MILES

KAUAI
NIIHAU
OAHU
Honolulu
MOLOKAI
MAUI
LANAI
KAHOOLAWE
Haleakala National Park
PACIFIC OCEAN
HAWAII
HAWAII VOLCANOES NATIONAL PARK

What is a Volcano?

A volcano is a hole where melted rock called magma comes up from inside the earth. As soon as magma is above ground, it's lava.

Volcano is also a word for the hill or mountain built by many eruptions of lava. But where does magma come from?

Scientists believe the earth has a very hot center about 7079 kilometers across. Surrounding this center, or core, is the mantle, a layer of rock about 2896 kilometers thick. Around the mantle is the earth's crust. On the big land masses, or continents, the crust is about 40 to 96 kilometers thick. Under the sea, the crust is only about five kilometers thick.

Coal miners know that the deeper you go into the earth, the hotter it gets. About 32 kilometers under the ground, it gets hot enough to melt rock. But usually rocks are under too much pressure to melt.

No one is sure how, but in some places the mantle melts and magma collects in chambers, or "hot spots." When the magma gets hot enough and full of gases, it flows toward cracks or holes where it can boil and rumble out as red hot lava, a volcanic eruption.

An Island is Born

Many scientists agree that the earth's crust is almost like a cracked shell on a boiled egg. Each broken piece of crust is called a "plate." All over the earth, these huge plates drift very slowly. Under the Pacific Ocean, the plate moves a few centimeters a year toward the northwest.

Deep in the earth's mantle beneath the mid-Pacific Ocean is a hot spot. During the last 100 million years, the Pacific plate moved over this magma chamber, and volcanic islands formed. Each island began with lava flowing out of a hole in the ocean floor. At times the volcano remained quiet, or dormant. Then it became active and erupted again. This happened over and over. Slowly, the volcano built a submarine mountain out of many layers of lava. The mountain grew until it rose above the sea. An island was born!

As the Pacific plate drifted, the first volcanic island moved away from the hot spot, and a new volcano formed to the southeast. Gradually, a chain of many islands formed. The last eight islands of this chain make up most of the state of Hawai'i: Ni'ihau, Kaua'i, O'ahu, Moloka'i, Lana'i, Maui, Kaho'olawe, and Hawai'i.

An Island Born Of Lava ▶

The
First Plants

The youngest of this chain of volcanic islands is Hawai'i. When you visit the national park, you may wonder how this land of lava became a land with plants and animals.

It's believed that a blue-green alga was the first plant to cling to the Hawaiian Islands. These algae, and later the spores of lichens, mosses, and ferns were carried by the wind. Growing, dying, and decaying, these pioneer plants mixed with cinder, ash, and weathered bits of lava to form soil where other plants could grow.

Carried by wind or water, every 20 or 30 thousand years, a new seed found its way to one of these tiny dots in a huge ocean. Over countless years, only about 275 kinds of flowering plants managed to arrive and live on the island chain. By the time the Big Island grew out of the sea, there were seeds and spores of many plants from nearby islands ready to island-hop to this new place.

Separated from the rest of the world, these plants developed, or evolved, into very special forms. Most of the native flowering plants and two thirds of the ferns are found *only* in Hawai'i.

pukupu Fern—A Pioneer Plant—Native Hawaiian

Silversword—Native Hawaiian Flowering Plant

The First Animals

With the nearest land 3800 kilometers away, it's a wonder any animals chanced to come to Hawai'i. But water and wind brought floating and flying forms of insect life or their eggs. Only 150 species of native insects survived.

One mammal, the hoary bat, may have been aided by the trade winds on its journey to Hawai'i. Another native mammal is the monk seal.

It's a long flight for land birds to come from the mainland. Did they find floating logs to rest on? Did strong winds speed their flight? One kind of honeycreeper bird made it to the islands. And from this one species, a family of 22 species evolved. Each one has a different shape of bill and its own way of behaving. The red 'i'iwi's long curved bill lets it reach into lobelia and other deep flowers for nectar. The palila has a short powerful bill for cracking seeds.

Because they have evolved different bills and special habits, several species can live together on a small island.

'wi—Native Hawaiian Bird

Palila—Hawaiian Native

Nene

One of the rarest birds in the world evolved in Hawai'i. A wild goose, the nene, has probably evolved from a Canadian goose that flew off course and landed here.

About 25,000 nene lived on the islands of Maui and Hawai'i before people from Europe and America, the "Westerners," settled here. While Hawaiians did not prize the goose for its feathers or meat, Westerners liked to eat them. And by 1911 the nene had become very rare.

In 1918, a man on the island of Hawai'i began to raise nene. Some of his birds flew away to the lava slopes of Mauna Loa. Today more nene are being raised in the park for later release.

Birdlovers of several countries have also raised nene to be taken to their other natural home in the crater of Haleakala National Park on Maui.

In Hawai'i Volcanoes National Park, nene lived on the slopes of Mauna Loa in meadows called *kipuka*. The "raised" nene have bands on their legs. If you see a flying flock of geese, look for the leg bands. Then be happy if you don't see bands. It means the nene were hatched in the wild. It could also mean the nene is going to survive!

ne—A Wild Goose

Nene—The Rarest Goose In The World

Legends

Early Hawaiians answered many big questions with legends, or stories. One tells how the world was created.

At first a male god, Ku, and a goddess, Haumea, clung to each other very tightly. Between them in the dark were the demigods, their children. The demigod Kane wanted to see light, so he pushed them apart.

Haumea, Mother Earth, shook with sobs when she saw her beloved Ku so far away above her. The demigods turned her face down so she couldn't see Ku. Then she shook just once in a while. Ku became Father Sky, and in Hawai'i, raindrops are his tears. He cries for his lover far below.

To make Ku happy, two demigods paddled a giant canoe to the edge of the world. They gathered stars in a basket and put them on Ku's body. Each star was placed where an island would be in the ocean below.

According to legend, the sea captain Hawai'i Loa's guide had a vision. The vision said to sail under the stars known as Makali'i to find seven jewels in the sea. And when they sailed under the stars you may know as Pleiades, or Seven Sisters, they found the Hawaiian Islands.

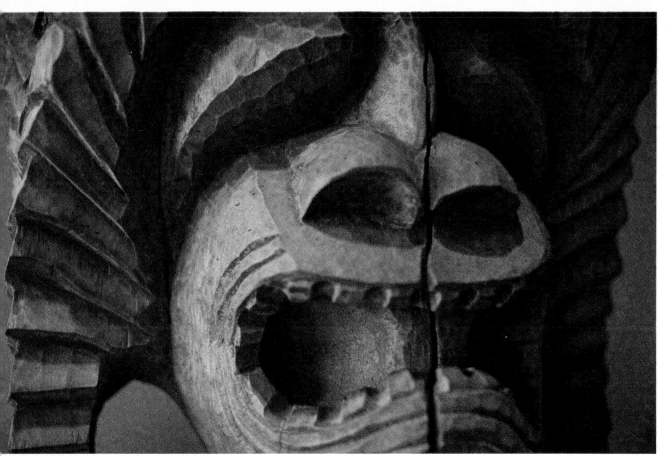

Some Gods Cry

These Islands Were Named For Hawai'i Loa

Some Gods Laugh

The First People

The first people to settle on these islands about A.D. 750 came from the Marquesas Islands. Using double-hulled canoes, these fine sailors followed the stars and "read" the sea. More than 3000 kilometers from their own land they discovered the Hawaiian Islands.

Not knowing what they would find, the early people brought coconuts, pigs, and small dogs. They built houses and temples of stone with thatched roofs.

About 500 years later, some bigger, stronger people came from Tahiti. They brought new gods with magic power, or *mana.* Priests, or *kahuna,* had new temples built where plants, animals, and even people were killed as sacrifices to the gods.

You can visit a temple, or *heiau,* at Hawai'i Volcanoes National Park. Remains of the Waha'ula Heiau are behind the Visitor Center in the coastal part of the park. Today at the Visitor Center, Hawaiians sing songs and show how they weave baskets and make the food, *poi.* They also tell stories and legends handed down from the early people.

page 24

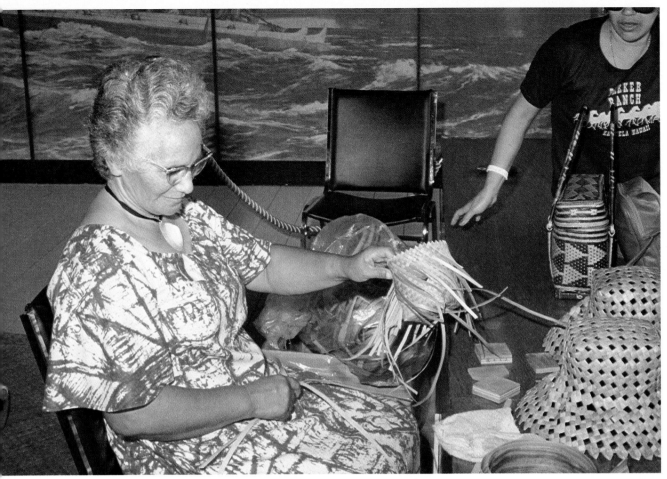

Weaving A Basket From Lauhala (Pandanus Leaves)

Taste Some Hawaiian Foods At Wahaʻula Heiau

The Legend of Pele

Hawaiian legends tell how Pele made all the craters on the islands. Pele is the goddess of fire, the daughter of Haumea and Ku.

Pele came to the Hawaiian Islands to get away from a cruel sister, goddess of the sea, Na Maka o Kaha'i.

First Pele went to Ni'ihau Island and dug a crater with a stick. But the sea goddess broke into the crater, so Pele ran away to Kaua'i. Pele made another crater home, but Na Maka chased her away from there, too.

Each time Pele made a new crater home, Na Maka tore at it with wind and crashing surf. At last, Pele found the big and high island of Hawai'i. Here she dug a deep, deep crater. And now Pele is safe from Na Maka o Kaha'i— or is she?

The goddess of fire has no peace, for she fears her sister the sea. Is this why Pele rages and roars, creates and destroys? To people, she appears sometimes as a wrinkled old hag. She demands not love, but respect. Hawaiians say, ''In Pele's home, you must step lightly, for you are on holy ground.''

The Work Of Pele—Kilauea Caldera, July, 1974 ▶

Kaha Ki'i- Petroglyphs

When you visit Hawai'i Volcanoes National Park, you can see the artwork of early Hawaiians. An area the size of a football field is covered with *kaha ki'i*, or petroglyphs. These are pictures carved in smooth lava near the ocean. At the end of a short hike, you can wander among hundreds of stone carvings. As you walk you may wonder why there are so many kaha ki'i in one place.

Who made the petroglyphs and when? Do the pictures tell the story of how the first people came? Or was this a "school" where people learned to "write?" Why do some kaha ki'i look like the Indian petroglyphs found in America?

The kaha ki'i field is at Pu'uloa, which means long hill. Some say people "signed" their pictures in the long hill to bring them long life.

Many of the kaha ki'i are circles with dots in the middle. Could they be volcanoes with craters? Perhaps the people chanted to Pele as they drew these, and begged her not to send red hot lava down the slopes above their villages. What do you think?

page 28

Nā Ki'i—Petroglyphs At Pu'uloa

Who "Signed" This Picture?

Your Visit to Hawai'i Volcanoes

A trip to any national park is always better if you know what to expect. If you read about the park, you can decide in advance how you want to spend your time. Write to the address on page 10 for a list of good books about the park.

The Visitor Center is the place to go as soon as you arrive. Here you can get a free map and see movies of some volcanic eruptions. A museum display explains volcanoes and shows some of the native plants and animals.

In summer you can get a schedule that tells about naturalist activities. Park naturalists are the people who lead nature walks and give evening talks.

On a nature walk, you'll learn how native plants are different from mainland varieties. Or you may go on a steamy crater walk and find out how one of the main volcanoes, Kilauea, has changed.

Color slides are shown with the evening talks. The slides may be about volcanoes, plants, animals, or the creatures that live in lava caves, or tubes. You'll leave these talks with a feeling that Hawai'i is a very special place.

sting 'Ohelo Berries On A Nature Walk

To Know a Volcano

After a volcano erupts, the top usually collapses, making a basin called a crater. If a crater is wider than 1.6 kilometers, it is a caldera.

Two hikes in this park will help you know a volcano. The Halemaʻumaʻu Trail takes you across the Kilauea Caldera. On this two-hour hike you pass a crater within the caldera. It's the summit crater, Halemaʻumaʻu, where a lake of lava sometimes rises and falls when Kilauea erupts.

You can also hike into Kilauea Iki, the crater on the side of the main volcano. The vent of Kilauea Iki erupted 16 times from November 14 to December 21, 1959. Lava fountains shot over 500 meters into the sky. The eruption spilled tons of lava into the crater. When the eruption stopped, much of that lava drained back into the vent.

When you hike across Kilauea Iki, you can expect steam to puff out of the cracks in the lava. But don't expect the vent to belch at you. If it were about to erupt, the trail would be closed. Piles of rocks called *ahu* mark the trail where it's safe to go, even in the mouth of a volcano.

page 32

Halemaʻumaʻu—Kilauea's Summit Crater

Kilauea Iki—1959

The Author In The "Mouth" Of A Volcano—Kilauea Iki

Who Knows a Volcano?

How do the scientists, called volcanologists know you are safe on a crater trail? At the edge of Kilauea is an observatory where dials, drums, gauges, and charts tell volcanologists what's happening to the earth's crust.

Instruments are planted all around the volcanoes. Electric signals go from these many points to the observatory.

Some of the instruments show if the earth above the magma is bulging. When the earth bulges, volcanologists begin to expect an eruption.

When magma expands with gas, it forces its way toward the surface and shakes the earth. The observatory has instruments that record every tremor, or shake, in the earth's crust.

When instruments in the observatory show a lot of tremors and bulges in one area, volcanologists can pretty well guess where an eruption might occur. Word goes out to the park rangers. They close off dangerous roads and trails. At the same time, park people try to keep some places open where visitors can see what they all hope to see when they visit this park, a volcanic eruption.

Instruments Warn Of Coming Eruptions

Needle Records Earth Tremors

Who Knows A Volcano?

Lava

Lava takes many forms and does strange things. When lava flows like thick cement and leaves a shiny, ropy surface, it's called *pahoehoe*. Sometimes pahoehoe flows around trees and sets them on fire. The lava cools and makes a mold of the tree before it burns away.

Some lava forms round droplets as it falls through the air. Often, as droplets fall from the top of a lava fountain, thin strands of glass spin off and become "Pele's hair." When the droplets are tear-shaped, they're called "Pele's tears."

At times a volcano ejects, or throws out, lava bombs, blobs bigger than baseballs. When lava spatters into a pile, it's a spatter cone.

If you think of early Hawaiians walking barefoot over rough, chunky lava, you can imagine why they named it *aa.*

In 1959, Kilauea Iki gushed pahoehoe into its crater. During the same eruption, the vent also belched out spongy bits of lava called cinder. The cinder piled up into a cone and covered a forest beyond the cone. When you hike the Devastation Trail, you walk across that burned-out forest.

Tree Mold

Beside Devastation Trail

Lava Tubes

When pahoehoe flows along, it may cool on the surface. This insulates the very hot lava beneath the surface, so it keeps flowing. When the supply of lava is gone, a tunnel, or empty tube, is left.

You can walk through a big one of these, the Thurston Lava Tube, when you visit Hawai'i Volcanoes. It's in the 'Ohi'a-fern Forest on Crater Rim Drive.

Thurston Lava Tube is a short walk open to the public. But some lava tubes are much longer, darker, and wetter. They are deep caves where small worlds of creatures have evolved. Some tiny animals live on plant roots that grow down through the tops of the tubes. Those animals are eaten by other animals, and some even live on the droppings of other species.

In 1971, scientists began to study the cave life in lava tubes. They have found unusual spiders, blind fish, and crickets. Because these creatures evolved on the islands over thousands of years, lava tube animals are like no other animals in the world.

Pahoehoe Flow At Mauna Ulu—January, 1974

Thurston Lava Tube

Nature Walks

Volcanoes are exciting and fun to explore, but leave time to do and see more. Check the park schedule in summer so you won't miss a nature walk on the 'Ili-ahi (Sandalwood) Trail. You'll find out that while Hawaiian plants evolved through thousands of years, Hawai'i had only bats, birds, and a few insects before people arrived. There were no big animals to eat or trample plants. For this reason, Hawai'i's native plants have no thorns, poisons, or other forms of protection.

You might want to frown at the "bad guys": tritonia, fuchsia, ginger, and orchids. These are non-natives that escaped from people's gardens and spread all over Hawai'i. Now they take up space that some people feel should be saved for truly Hawaiian plants.

After a nature walk, you can walk into the 'Ohi'a-fern Forest and name that giant fern towering over your head. It's the hapu'u. Then if you stand still and listen, you may hear an 'apapane as it flits among the red blooms of the 'ohi'a tree.

And be sure to take the self-guided trail through Kipuka Puaulu, or Bird Park, a natural "showcase" of Hawaiian plants.

ōhi‘a-Fern Forest

Loop Trail In Bird Park

Drives and Other Hikes

Maybe the first drive you'll take is on Crater Rim Road. It goes all around the rim of Kilauea Caldera. Chain of Craters Road takes you past new eruptions and by prehistoric pit craters. Parking areas along these roads make it easy to get out, take pictures, or even hike a bit.

Late in the day is a good time to follow Hilina Pali Road to the end. Looking over the pali, or cliff, you can see the ocean below. This part of the island dropped suddenly during an earthquake in 1975. It caused a huge tidal wave, or *tsunami*, that engulfed people who were camping on the beach. The miracle was that only two of them lost their lives.

When you've had enough driving, it's time to hike. All of Crater Rim Trail takes a whole day, but you can also walk just part of it. The toughest trek is Mauna Loa. For an overnight hike, you must register at park headquarters. On Mauna Loa, you can camp in shelters or stay in cabins at Red Hill and the Summit.

Hikers Follow Trail Markers On Mauna Loa ▶

The Tears of Ku

Legend says that when Ku was separated from his lover, Haumea, he cried many tears. Maybe he is still crying. Almost every day his tears fall on the islands.

Mountains built by Pele's fiery lava also help cause the rain. Trade winds from the northeast pick up water vapor from the sea. Vapor turns to rainclouds as it rises over Pele's lava mounds.

These clouds drop most of their rain on the eastern slopes, so the kona, or western, coast sits in a "rain shadow." At the Visitor Center on the eastern slope of Kilauea, the average yearly rainfall is about 2.5 meters. A few kilometers to the west, the Observatory sits in a rain shadow. Only a little over a meter of rain falls there each year.

Ku's tears beat down on the mountains, cut canyons, and carry bits of lava to the lowlands. Here the water helps pioneer plants build soil and the island becomes a rich green jewel in the sea.

In this land of expectations, you may or may not see Pele's fury. But you will see the tears of Ku. And as his tears cling to 'ohelo leaves and berries, you may recall the legends as well as the real stories of how Hawai'i Volcanoes National Park came to be.

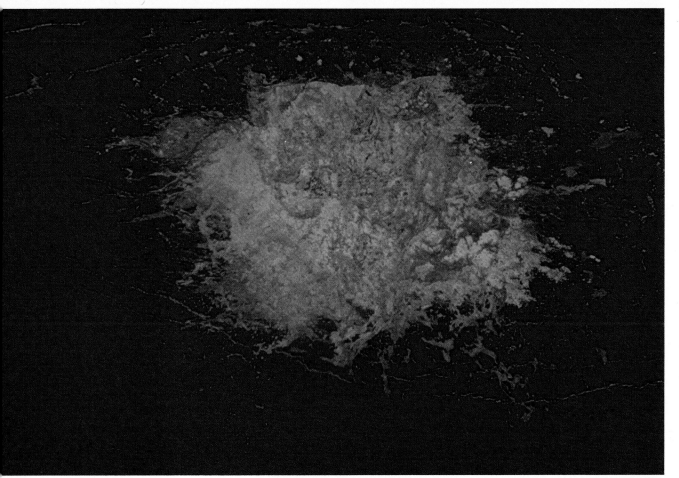

Halemaʻumaʻu—September, 1974

Ku's Tears Cling To ʻOhelo Leaves And Berries

Another National Park in Hawai'i

Haleakala National Park holds another volcanic experience for you on the island of Maui.

People named this giant mountaintop "bowl" a crater. But it's really the joining of two deep valleys that cut into the mountain. After the valleys formed, volcanic eruptions covered much of the valleys with lava and cinders. Within this craterlike basin are pahoehoe, aa, cinder cones, lava bombs, lava flows, and lava tubes for you to explore.

Well prepared with warm clothes, sun hats, and water, strong hikers like to cross this astronauts' training ground. Depending on how much you want to see, you can day hike or get a permit to stay in the crater overnight.

The last eruption of Haleakala Volcano was in 1790, outside the present park area. But since that's just a "short time ago" in the story of the earth, this is called a dormant volcanic area. So far, no one calls Haleakala an extinct volcano.

You can get more information and a reading list from the Superintendent, Haleakala National Park, P.O. Box 537, Makawao, Maui, Hawai'i 96768.

leakala National Park

The Author and Illustrators

Wyoming-born Ruth Radlauer's love affair with national parks began in Yellowstone. During her younger years, she spent her summers in the Bighorn Mountains, in Yellowstone, or on Casper Mountain.

Ed and Ruth Radlauer, graduates of the University of California at Los Angeles, are authors of many books for young people. Along with their adult daughter and sons, they photograph and write about a wide variety of subjects ranging from monkeys to motorcycles.

The Radlauers live in California, where Ruth and Ed spend most of their time in the mountains near Los Angeles.